Sold In Sixty Seconds™

The Local Advertiser's Guide To Winning With Jingles

by
Ann McWilliams and David Mayo

authorHOUSE™

1663 LIBERTY DRIVE, SUITE 200
BLOOMINGTON, INDIANA 47403
(800) 839-8640
WWW.AUTHORHOUSE.COM

AuthorHouse™
1663 Liberty Drive, Suite 200
Bloomington, IN 47403
www.authorhouse.com
Phone: 1-800-839-8640

AuthorHouse™ UK Ltd.
500 Avebury Boulevard
Central Milton Keynes, MK9 2BE
www.authorhouse.co.uk
Phone: 08001974150

First published by AuthorHouse 1/26/2006

ISBN: 1-4208-5261-2 (sc)

Printed in the United States of America
Bloomington, Indiana

This book is printed on acid-free paper.

ACKNOWLEDGMENTS

This book would not have been possible without the experience and input of many people and companies over the past decades. We wish to acknowledge their contributions and to say "Thank you" for all of the wisdom, insight and effort they've helped us to gain through the years.

Tom DiNoto, founder of Tuesday Productions, is a constant source of inspiration and support. We are grateful for his advice and expertise and we truly believe nobody is better at this business.

Henry DeVries and Denise Bryson at New Client Marketing Institute took our experience and ideas and helped us to turn them into the book you're reading today. We deeply appreciate their guidance and assistance.

For many years Patti Zlaket was Tuesday's creative maven, and her expertise contributed enormously to the development of this book. We could not have written the book without her, and we wish her all the success in the world.

Lori Quest's creative input throughout the process of writing this book gave us a great title. Thank you, Lori.

Our clients offer us daily opportunities to apply, extend and refine our craft. We especially appreciate all those whom we've mentioned in this book and who keep us informed of how their jingle is helping them to win in their market.

Finally, there are many national advertisers whose outstanding jingle work over the past 100 years creates a living textbook for the student willing to look for, crystallize and apply their lessons. Each company and brand mentioned in this book owns its own trademarks, and inclusion in this book is not intended to appropriate ownership or diminish their marks. Thanks to Target, Tropicana, J.C. Penney, Marlboro, Carnival Cruises, Audi, Cadillac, Chevy, Chiquita, McDonald's, Pepsi, Campbell's, General Motors, Oscar Mayer, Wrigley's, Winston, Coca Cola, Brylcreem, Rolls-Royce, Sears, Pepperidge Farms, General Foods International Coffees, Ford, Klondike, DeBeers, Nokia, Harley-Davidson, Intel, Windows, Chili's, Almond Joy, Big Red, CrackerJack, Spaghettios, Bosco, Kit-Kat, Hershey, Roto-Rooter, Moss Security, Wyborowa, Pioneer, The Economist, Range Rover, Holiday Inn, Casio, Weight Watchers, British Steel,

First National Bank of Chicago, Kodak, Ritz, John Deere, Mumm's, Money Magazine, Absolut, IBM, Citibank, Cutty Sark, Campari, Wal-Mart, Buick, Ferrari, Jeep, Oldsmobile, Wheaties, Cliquot, NBC, Alka Seltzer, Kellogg, Mary Kay, Exxon, Kentucky Fried Chicken, Jack in the Box, Hertz, Nike, Wendy's, Burger King, Adidas, Clairol, Toyota, Anheuser-Busch, Seagrams, Lincoln-Mercury, BMW, Acura, Circuit City, Levi's, Reebok, Pillsbury and Microsoft.

Finally, we stand on the shoulders of the authors and scholars who have made the science of musical advertising their field of inquiry.

CONTENTS

CHAPTER 1: SOLD IN SIXTY SECONDS

What, No Jingle?

Ah, the humble jingle. Those irresistibly catchy little ditties can stick in your head for years, and we'll prove it to you throughout this book.

If you advertise locally on radio or television, you really should understand and harness the musical memory power of the jingle to sell you and your business. In the era of ever-encroaching mega-chains and national competition, nothing can put you at the top of customers' minds like a jingle can. We'll get to *why* in a moment.

The longest jingle you'll usually ever hear lasts just :60 (sixty seconds). That might not seem like much time, but do this exercise: Check your watch or look at the clock on your computer. Now start timing. Sit there. For a full 60 seconds.

Sixty seconds is a long time—time to tell the key to your entire story. And a jingle can make your story memorable.

According to journalist Greg Haymes, a good commercial jingle becomes a kind of "soundtrack" for your life, just like the ever-evolving hit records on the top 10 pop charts. "The key characteristics are that they're simple, catchy and have enjoyed high exposure levels over a period of many years," says Haymes. "That describes a number of pop hit records, but it's also a fair definition of a jingle." Be honest: Sometime, somewhere, with a group of friends, somebody started singing or humming a jingle from the good old days. And you joined right in.

Who Can Forget These Jingles?

> **Rice-A-Roni**
> **the San Francisco treat**
>
> **For all you do**
> **this Bud's for you.**
>
> **We're American Airlines**
> **something special in the air**

We are especially proud of those particular jingles because our company, Tuesday Productions, created and produced arrangements of them. The fact that so many Americans can still sing those songs is one of the things that we love about our work. On a local level, many people in southern California can never forget "You won't get a lemon at Toyota of Orange"—one of our jingles that's been on the air for over 30 years.

We are often asked, "What makes a good jingle?"

A jingle that can get your product or service "sold in 60 seconds" marries the right mood, a memorable melody and a perfect positioning statement.

Some people have described the perfect jingle as a lyric that rolls off your tongue without any effort, a tune that you whistle as you walk down the street long after the jingle is aired.

The jingle's job is to provide an arresting sound that grabs and holds immediate audience attention. It hones in on their wants and needs, makes them aware your business is an option to fulfill those wants and needs. Best of all, it sticks in their mind until they're ready to make the purchase.

Great jingles also become a *mnemonic,* which Encarta defines as "a short rhyme, phrase, or other mental technique for making information easier to memorize." Some mnemonics use initials to help people remember a long series of words ("My Very Energetic Mother Just Served Us Nine Pizzas" is a mnemonic device for remembering the names of the planets in the order they orbit the sun—Mercury, Venus, Earth, Mars, Jupiter, Saturn, Uranus, Neptune, Pluto). Jingles are also mnemonics: "Plop Plop Fizz Fizz Oh What A Relief It Is" has become a mnemonic for Alka-Seltzer.

Not Everyone Loves Jingles

Especially in the past few years, some people have suggested that jingles are passé. Studies show that jingle usage is on the decline. National jingles like, "You'll wonder where the yellow went when you brush your teeth with Pepsodent," or "For all you do… this Bud's for you" are no longer in vogue.

Instead, it seems, many companies are paying big bucks to "borrow" pop music, using the latest radio hits to try to sell their products and services.

Critics of jingles also occasionally suggest that, even if jingles *do* work, they are too expensive for local advertisers. But this is the product of miscalculated thinking. The evidence that jingles *can* sell in sixty seconds is unassailable. Repetition and continuity of image and message, in fact, are two cornerstones of good marketing, and a long-lived jingle is one of the very best ways to achieve both affordably.

The fact is, if you measure increased sales over the jingle's broadcast life to its initial production and licensing costs, it often requires an investment of just pennies per day. Some radio stations and local cable companies are willing to offer advertisers "credit" toward their initial jingle production costs, awarding jingle buyers free airtime over the course of a long-term contract. Why do you think they do that? Because they know advertisers with jingles have committed to a long-term competitive strategy that helps them to compete. Committed advertisers are the most likely to be successful advertisers—and that's what broadcasters want most.

Maybe you, as a business owner in a small to midsized local market, reason that a great jingle would help you, but you can't afford the rates a Madison Avenue advertising agency would charge you for a great slogan set to song. If so, that's not unusual. Many local advertisers are not aware that, through exclusive music licensing, they can obtain customized jingles at a fraction of the cost.

The fact remains that currently, a great deal of national commercials today feature popular songs rather than custom-written jingles. Perhaps you've heard:

- The late Roy Orbison's "You Got It" for Target®.
- Olivia Newton-John's "Physical" for Tropicana® orange juice.
- JC Penney's® pitching its spring fashion line with Fine Young

Cannibals' "She Drives Me Crazy."

- Bob Seger's "Like a Rock" embodying the idea of Chevy Trucks.

Using pop or rock music in national spots is not exactly a new trend. Elmer Bernstein's "Theme From the Magnificent Seven," originally penned as a cowboy movie theme, was licensed to Marlboro® cigarettes for its "cowboy" commercials for years. By incorporating a familiar bit of pop music into their advertisements, huge national businesses bank on the added value of instant recognition with listeners. The cost of doing so is staggering. But that's not the biggest problem.

When advertisers use music that consumers already know, they always risk the problem of the *song itself*—not their *product*—taking center stage. Take a look back at the list above. Did you put the "hit song" together with the right advertiser? We bet not. Even Chevy's recently-retired "Like A Rock" campaign, which ran consistently for over a decade, was typically associated with Chevrolet in general—not Chevy Trucks in particular.

Then there are the costs of using existing music. Estimates of fees required to license music from Led Zeppelin (Cadillac®) or Bob Seger (Chevy® trucks) range from the high six figures to several million dollars. Those fees make no sense whatsoever to a local advertiser.

Even worse are the costs of using music without a proper license. In some very small markets, broadcast stations may not be aware of the implications of copyright law. Some small-market broadcasters occasionally "sample" a popular tune and use it in local ads. But this is an unwise choice for any business—or station. Fact is, if somebody uses music without a proper license and permission *and they're caught,* fines can reach into the tens— even hundreds—of thousands of dollars. In this post-Napster era, copyright holders are vigorously defending their intellectual property even more.

We know of one local advertiser who "borrowed" a tune without permission to whip up what he thought would be a "cheap" jingle. By the time it was all over, the advertiser was sued by the song's copyright holder, found guilty of infringement and ordered to pay not only thousands of dollars in damages, but also *all* the court costs. That "cheap" $500 jingle ended up costing the business well over $100,000.

The upshot for local advertisers is that having a radio station "sample" a few seconds of Creed or Madonna or Travis Tritt becomes a lot less appealing when the penalties for getting caught are really understood.

As we said earlier, another problem with appropriating a pop tune for your advertisements goes deeper than the price of licensing (or the prohibitive penalties for *not* licensing). It's that if people already know the song, they won't necessarily link it with *you* or *your business*. Be honest: When you hear Cyndi Lauper's "Girls Just Wanna Have Fun," do you think of any particular product or service? How about David Bowie's "Rebel Rebel?" (Bowie, incidentally, began his career as a jingle singer).

Both of these songs were featured in very expensive national campaigns. We'll even tell you what industries: Cyndi was hawking cruises and David was singing about cars. If you actually did link "Girls Just Wanna Have Fun" with Carnival® Cruises (not Princess, not Holland America) and "Rebel, Rebel" with Audi® (not Toyota, not Nissan, not Volkswagen), you did better than most people. That's because if people already know the music, it's much, much harder to re-wire their brains to associate a commercial offering with the tune. In most cases, you're better off creating a unique audio brand from scratch—a jingle that's uniquely you.

Local Licensing To The Rescue

When it comes to smaller markets and local advertising, there's a catch. Most local advertisers simply can't afford to license music from a pop, rock or country superstar (Microsoft® paid $12 Million to use the Rolling Stones' "Start Me Up" when they rolled out Windows 95). Even if a local advertiser *could* afford it, it's likely that the artist still wouldn't want to license the tune to a local advertiser—after all, if a tune is licensed for use in Seattle, then it can't be sold to a big national chain whose ads would run all over the place, including Seattle. Better to hold out for the big national license. Finally, tally up the cost of re-recording the tune into a viable :60 or :30 format, and snagging the latest Britney hit becomes virtually impossible.

But local advertisers can still license commercial music. (They can get a singer who sounds a lot like Britney, too, if they work with a production company that draws from a wide talent pool.) With this approach, you can produce, license and record a local market jingle based on a professional music track that sounds like it came right off of Madison Avenue for just a few thousand dollars.

The biggest problem with local advertising today is there is so much of it. Consumers are assaulted from many different angles. While you can't afford not to advertise, you absolutely can't afford not to be memorable (please pardon the quadruple negative, but we feel very strongly about this point).

Read on to learn all the power of the humble jingle. When you make it simple, then you've made it memorable and will make the most of your advertising investment. That's what jingles have done since radio and television first hit the airwaves. That's what they can do for you right now.

CHAPTER 2: MUSIC AND MEMORY

No matter how old you are now, you grew up hearing jingles—songs that feature lyrics about a company, product or service played in the broadcast (and now, online) media. From the earliest days of radio, businesses large and small have used the power of music to reach out and touch customers. It was 1926, in fact, when the first commercial jingle, for Wheaties, went out over the airwaves.

If you're like most people, some of your earliest memories correlate strongly with music.

Mary had a little lamb,
Little lamb,
Little lamb
Mary had a little lamb
Whose fleece
Was white as snow...

- Quickly, try to think back: Did you know what "fleece" was when you first learned this song?

- If you didn't know what "fleece" was, did it matter? Could you still sing the song?

- Did you learn all the words anyway?

- Are those words still with you?

- What's the next verse?

Now, *Mary Had A Little Lamb* is not a jingle, to be sure, but it's structured much the same as the best jingles. It's short, it's repetitive, it's got a simple melody that's easy to remember and easier to sing along to. This simple little song demonstrates a lot about how music works with the human mind to create memories—even memories of things we don't quite understand.

The reason most Americans can remember details about Mary and her baby sheep or Georgie Porgie who kissed the girls and made them cry, is this: *Music has a special ability to penetrate the human brain—to take information and wrap it in a package that makes it almost impossible to forget.* Producers of children's shows know this. Music is one of the main tools used by educational broadcasters since the advent of television.

In the late 1960s and early 1970s, groundbreaking children's shows like *Sesame Street, The Electric Company* and *Mister Rogers' Neighborhood* used what educators had known for years about music. Setting something to a tune makes it far easier to teach children subjects that are shockingly complex or difficult.

Don't believe that? Ask somebody who's "thirtysomething" to recite the Preamble to the United States Constitution. Chances are, if you run into somebody in that age group who can do so, she or he will *sing* it to you—to a tune that was learned when it played in the 1970s, mixed into commercials between Saturday morning cartoons. The short, popular cartoon called *Schoolhouse Rock* set all manner and sorts of difficult subjects to music— history, math, civics, even grammar. As a result, "Conjunction junction, what's your function?" is a question that most of the youth of that era can still answer today. The same person who answers your question with a ditty that begins "We The People Of the United States, In Order To Form a More Perfect Union… " can probably also tell you how a law is made if you give them this hint: "I'm just a bill. I'm only a bill. And I'm sitting here on Capitol Hill."

CHAPTER 3: MUSIC THAT TEACHES

It may be a difficult thing to believe, but in 1944, a banana was an exotic thing. The strange tropical fruit required handling that was different from many fruits that North American housewives were used to. It didn't behave like apples or pears or oranges. It needed special treatment. The Chiquita® Banana company, which imported the fruit, needed to teach American housewives how to properly ripen and prepare bananas for their family. Legend has it, the Chiquita Banana song was written around a piano while the advertising team used a box of paper clips for maracas.

Fifty years later, the basic tune is still used in Chiquita's advertising. The original lyrics were straightforward and they accomplished their mission.

Jingle Break

I'm Chiquita banana
and I've come to say
Bananas have to ripen
in a certain way
When they are flecked with brown
and have a golden hue
Bananas taste the best
and are best for you
You can put them in a salad
You can put them in a pie
Any way you want to eat them
It's impossible to beat them
But, bananas like the climate
of the very, very tropical equator
So you should never put bananas
in the refrigerator.

The Chiquita® Banana Company

The jingle ran 376 times a day on radio stations across the country. Did it work? A recent survey revealed that in the United States, 98% of people know what Chiquita sells. That makes Chiquita Bananas one of the most recognized brands on earth.

As we move on through this book, we'll take a few time outs to remind you of classic national broadcast jingles, some of which you haven't heard in ten, twenty, maybe even thirty years, and we're willing to bet that you'll remember not only the words, but also the tune, and most importantly, the name of the sponsor.

That's what winning in advertising is all about.

No matter what you call them—commercial music, musical branding or just plain jingles—these musical tools can lend a huge boost to your local marketing and advertising efforts.

CHAPTER 4: MUSIC THAT SELLS—A BRIEF HISTORY OF JINGLES

The use of music and entertainment to promote products and sell services dates all the way back to the early 20th century, when Esso Gasoline sponsored the Guy Lombardo Orchestra and required a receipt for their gasoline to be admitted to shows. In 1908, Johnny Marks recorded a little ditty called "In My Merry Oldsmobile," and it didn't take long for the automaker in question to adopt the song for its own promotional and advertising purposes. (This is one of the rare times that buying the rights to a popular song made sense!)

The first "real" jingle, written solely for use in radio advertising to make the product name memorable, hit in 1926. A new horizon opened to advertisers with the words "Have you tried Wheaties, the best breakfast food in the land?" The jingle played in very few of the earliest radio markets, but where it *did* play, consumption of Wheaties soared. Unfortunately, for reasons that have never been clear, the jingle never made it into wider release. Perhaps it was simply ahead of its time.

In 1941, "Pepsi Cola Hits The Spot" became the first widely distributed and played jingle, with more than a million copies pressed just for jukeboxes. The same year, "I'm a Chiquita Banana" moved *Time* magazine to name it "The undisputed No. 1 on the jingle-jangle hit parade." The jingle craze was in full swing.

In the following decades, jingles transformed the nature of broadcast advertising. Exploiting the natural ease of memorizing music and lyrics, companies sang the praises of everything from cigarettes to chocolate milk and paved the way for the increasing commercialization of "real" music.

By the 1980s, baby boomer nostalgia led to odd retro-jingle hybrids, in which familiar tunes were overlaid with new lyrics. Thus, Jerry Lee Lewis' music was reborn for Burger King's "Whole Lotta Breakfast Going On" and the Platters original tune "Only You" transformed into "Only Wendy's." While some artists held out, refusing to "sell out" to commercial interests, by early 2000, many artists were happy to supplement their CD royalties by licensing music to advertisers.

Still, when you ask people to sing a jingle, chances are they're going to come up with a song that was written specifically to promote a product—not "Start Me Up," the Rolling Stones tune that was used to introduce Windows

95, or the Beatles' "Revolution," which Nike licensed from Michael Jackson (who owns the Fab Four's catalog) in 1985—much to the dismay of fans and surviving Beatles alike.

Jingle Break: The Champions

Top 10 American Jingles of the 20th Century

1. You deserve a break today (McDonald's®)

2. Be all that you can be (United States Army)

3. Pepsi Cola hits the spot (Pepsi®)

4. M'mm, m'mm good (Campbell's®)

5. See the USA in your Chevrolet (General Motors®)

6. I wish I were an Oscar Mayer wiener (Oscar Mayer®)

7. Double your pleasure, double your fun (Wrigley's® Doublemint gum)

8. Winston tastes good like a cigarette should (Winston®)

9. It's the Real Thing (Coca Cola®)

10. Brylcreem®-- A little dab'll do ya

Source: www.adage.com

Ogilvy On Jingles

David Ogilvy set up shop on Madison Avenue in 1949. What started as a little creative boutique in New York grew to become one of the four largest advertising agencies in the world. According to *Time* magazine, he became "the most sought-after wizard in the advertising business" through campaigns for such clients as Rolls-Royce®, Sears® and Pepperidge Farms®.

Ogilvy shared his wizardry in 1963 by writing *Confessions of An Advertising Man,* followed in 1983 by *Ogilvy on Advertising.* "I am sometimes attacked for imposing 'rules.' Nothing could be further from the truth," wrote Ogilvy. "I *hate* rules. All I do is report on how consumers react to different stimuli. I may say to a copywriter, 'Research shows that commercials with celebrities are below average in persuading people to buy products. Are you *sure* you want to use a celebrity.' Call that a *rule?* Or I might say to an art director, 'Research suggests that if you set the copy in black type on a white background, more people will read it than if you set it in white type on a black background.' A *hint*, perhaps, but scarcely a rule."

What were Ogilvy's hints when it came to jingles? "Never use a jingle without trying it on people who have not read your script," wrote Ogilvy. "If they cannot decipher the words, don't put your jingle on the air."

He also had hints for broadcast advertising in general:

- Identify your brand early in the commercial.

- Identify it often.

- Promise the listener a benefit early in the commercial.

- Repeat it often.

CHAPTER 5: SO, WHY DO JINGLES WORK?

Before we dig deeper into how to make a jingle work for you in your local market, let's go over the primary reasons jingles work.

Memory

It's amazing that many songs you haven't heard in years will instantly come back to you... both words and melody. Setting a message to music is the quickest, most reliable way to get that message remembered. How else could a two-year-old remember something as difficult as 26 letters of the alphabet?

Music is a tool used by almost every teacher, at every grade level. It can help teach children and teenagers the basics of everything from language and science to mathematics, and it is even used by instructors who teach English as a second language to adults.

The same "memory magic" can be used to teach your local market just about anything you want them to know. Don't believe it? Do you remember the ingredients of a Big Mac?

Jingle Break

Two All-Beef Patties
Special Sauce
Lettuce
Cheese
Pickles
Onions
On a Sesame Seed Bun

McDonald's®

Why did McDonald's feel the need to run this ad?

The Big Mac cost more than other fast-food burgers being sold at the time, and certainly more than all other McDonald's burgers. It had been introduced in 1968, but until the "two all beef patties..." jingle, consumers had been a bit unclear about why they should pay more for a hamburger. In 1974, McDonald's answered that question, and people all over North America could suddenly tell you *exactly* how much stuff was piled onto that sesame seed bun. Big Macs, to this day, remain a staple of the McDonald's menu, thirty years after the launch of the jingle.

Chapter 6: The Subconscious

Music works both on the conscious level—the part of the brain that is busy seeing and hearing and tasting and processing every second of every day—and on the *subconscious* level, where mental work that you don't even know about is going on. You may not realize you're absorbing a song until, suddenly, you've got the latest pop hit *stuck in your head and it won't go away.* (Don't you hate it when that happens?)

No other form of advertising sticks with people the way jingles do, because no other form of advertising incorporates this ability of music to touch and enter the subconscious.

All forms of media have their uses, of course, and the best local marketers know how to mix it up. When you're trying to beat the competition, it always pays to use as many tools as you can afford.

If your aim is to deliver a mountain of precise, detailed information about a current sale or promotion or your new product line or the myriad of merchandise that just came in, then a print ad is probably best suited to your specific ad goals. But if you want to get the name of your business out there in the community and make sure consumers will remember you when they need you, nothing beats music.

Nothing.

If you're a Baby Boomer or even one of the older members of Generation X, you probably remember these great brands and taglines.

- If it says Libby's Libby's Libby's on the label label label you will like it like it like it on your table table table

- Here's to good friends, tonight is kind of special. The beer we'll pour must say something more, so tonight, let it be Lowenbrau

- Double your pleasure, double your fun with Wrigley's Doublemint gum

- Mmm, mmmm, good... mmmm mmmmm good... that's what Campbell's Soups are, mmmmm mmmmm good.

You probably can't remember what was in the grocery store's sale circular last night. So why can you remember those brand names, and even the emotional feeling that the original ads evoked? The difference is music, which reached past your critical conscious mind and touched your subconscious. Music drummed those brand names and companies into your mind. *Permanently.*

You can do the same for your business.

CHAPTER 7: EMOTION

Just about anybody who's ever gotten misty-eyed hearing a few strains of "our song" a few months after a breakup knows the truth. Music taps deep into the emotional centers of the brain and the heart. It's as though the combination of rhythm, melody, instruments, voice and lyrics somehow make a magical potion that does what none of them could ever do alone.

In local advertising and marketing, a really good jingle—music that sinks in and sets your business apart from the competition—is the difference between black and white and color in print advertising. If the music you're using now in your local radio and cable TV advertising isn't stirring emotions, it isn't doing its job. If you aren't using music, you aren't tapping into the deep, visceral power of music to position yourself in the mind of your potential customer… yet. That's not unusual, and it's OK.

By the time you've finished reading this book, you'll know exactly how to combine all the right elements to create a musical image that's perfect for branding your business. Music can portray the full spectrum of feelings. Which ones do you want associated with your business? The "fit" of emotion with the business's image is an important point to consider. No matter what kind of music the business owner likes, it's critical to match the emotional content of music with the business itself. That may mean choosing music that differs from the owner's personal preferences. After all, a baker might love R&B music, but unless the bakery is in a geographic region where people associate bread and cookies with sexy, sultry, seductive emotions, the owner's preferred music doesn't necessarily match the kinds of emotions a bakery needs to stir (no pun intended).

☑ A Checklist: What Emotions Should Your Jingle Evoke?

Optimism	Happiness
Melancholy	Hope
Sadness	Patriotism
Sexiness	Suspense
Romance	Sincerity
Joyousness	Contentment
Excitement	Determination
_____	_____

Chapter 8: Jingles People Love: Success Stories

> ## Jingle Break
>
> **I'd Like To Teach**
> **The world to sing**
> **In perfect harmony**
> **I'd like to buy the world a**
> **Coke**
> **And keep it company**
>
> *Coca-Cola®*

If you were around in 1971, you probably remember a song called "I'd Like To Teach The World To Sing" by the New Seekers. Did you remember the song began its life as a jingle for Coca-Cola? Somehow, "I'd Like To Teach The World To Sing" made you want to be a better person. The jingle's sentiments and the emotion behind the music built up such a popular following it soon became a pop hit in its own right. It sold a lot of Coke® and a lot of 45-rpm records, too. Hard to believe that the original spot has been off the air for more than three decades.

Surprisingly, good jingles have this effect even today. A jingle we worked on for the Wichita Convention Center and Visitor's Bureau board struck the same kind of nerve. We heard from the radio stations running the ads that they were receiving calls requesting "that new song, 'If you haven't been to Wichita lately, you haven't been to Wichita at all.'"

We also produced a Public Service Announcement, "Keep Idaho Green," intended to spread awareness of what the public can do to prevent forest fires. It was a very uplifting arrangement that sounded like people gathered around a campfire. (And yes, they smothered the coals before retiring for the night!) It began with one singer, eventually joined in by another voice, then another, until an entire group was singing—a real Kumbaya moment.

The spot ran on local stations as a "full sing" spot, all lyrics for 60 seconds—something that's rarely done nowadays. (Can you remember the last time a local advertiser had the nerve to just let you hum along and *didn't try to cram in a voiceover*?)

The result was incredible. People started calling into their local stations requesting the jingle. In this case, they *knew it was an advertisement*, and they didn't care! They liked the song so much, they were willing to ask to hear an advertisement again!

When's the last time somebody begged you for a copy of your last newspaper ad?

Even today, a well-crafted jingle can still make people want to hear it.

CHAPTER 9: COMPETE OR GET BEAT

In almost all retail businesses, and even in some service companies, one trend is clear from the last few years. The large national chain retailers have made it nearly impossible for small, independent, local businesses to compete based on price alone. That trend shows no sign of reversing, either, although some municipalities in the last few years have begun to organize opposition when a mega-chain announces plans to open a store in town.

Meanwhile, Mom-and-Pop stores struggle to find new and unique ways to bring in customers. Many have turned to offering high-end brands that aren't available at the super chains or specialized lines of merchandise. But changes in product offerings or focus often carry with them enormous risk, as well. What if nobody knows you're offering the new and better stuff? How can you make people understand that price isn't everything?

You first need to understand *how and why people buy.*

Chapter 10: Imagery Transfer—The Power of Media Synergy

When you hear the opening strains of John Williams' *Star Wars* theme, or "Thus Spake Zarathustra" (used by Stanley Kubrick to open his opus, *2001: A Space Odyssey*), chances are you "see" a visual from those movies in your mind's eye.

If you watched MTV in its early days, then it's likely that when you hear the first notes of Dire Straits' "Money For Nothing," you "see" the music video in your head. When you hear a radio ad for Budweiser that uses their fanfare music, you probably "see" a team of powerful Clydesdales trotting in the sunset or galloping through powdery snow.

You don't actively try to recall these visual images. They come into your mind unbidden, automatically, as a hard-wired response…to music.

The phenomenon of *imagery transfer* is at work in each of these cases. Imagery Transfer is a phenomenon that's been well researched and documented by perceptual psychologists and marketing scholars. In a nutshell, imagery transfer happens when the human brain comes to associate one sensory impression (like the sound of a particular piece of music) with another sensory impression (like a visual image).

Imagery transfer can work with other senses, too—the smell of apple pie conjuring up Grandma's face, or a print advertisement that brings to mind the company's jingle.

Studies have shown imagery transfer is incredibly powerful. In fact, according to a recent study, three out of four reported that they "see" a television commercial in their mind's eye *when they hear a radio ad that used the same music*. That means that for the cost of the radio ad, an advertiser essentially gets two messages across—the auditory message that radio is delivering, and a visual message that's playing entirely in the listener's mind—for free.

The Ear Beats The Eye

It's interesting that many people (erroneously) believe that the visual channel is the most direct way to get a message across. If that were true, we'd all remember everything we've ever read. We don't, of course. Even things we've read a number of times—like a favorite book or bedtime story—isn't planted as deeply in the subconscious mind as something that's been heard—like a song or a nursery rhyme.

Researchers have found, in fact, that it takes the mind more to process a printed word (180 milliseconds, to be precise) than a word that's spoken (140 milliseconds). The difference in time seems to be a short period when the mind is *translating* the printed word into a mental "sound" that the brain can "hear." Have you ever seen somebody moving their lips when they're reading? They're doing the same thing. They're translating the printed word to a spoken word, because the brain understands and retains sounds more easily than it does printed word.

Does this misconception about the eye vs. the ear hurt advertisers? Consider this. Consumers spend 85% of their time with sound-oriented media (radio and television), and only 15% of their time with exclusively eye-oriented media (like newspapers and magazines). Yet, puzzlingly, advertisers spend more than half of their budgets on print ads—the media that people spend the *least* amount of time with, and the media that makes it *most* difficult for consumers to absorb and remember!

Not surprisingly, research shows that if there's one key to successful use of imagery transfer in advertising, it's **consistent music**. If you invest in both television and radio, but don't use the same music in both, then it's less likely that listeners will "see" your television ad when they hear your radio spots. It takes a common thread—a "sonic brand"—to trigger the powerful cross-media synergies of imagery transfer.

If you work with an agency to design your campaign right, imagery transfer can significantly boost the results of *all* your ads in *all* your media. The key is sound—music and words together, in the form that the brain can absorb most easily. One unique, memorable, powerful jingle that listeners associate with you is the core element of an integrated branding and awareness campaign.

Even print ads, it turns out, benefit from imagery transfer. In one study, half of the people surveyed reported they "heard" a company's jingle when they saw the company's print advertisement.

Executed well, imagery transfer built on the cornerstone of a great jingle can help local advertisers get more bang for their advertising buck.

Sonic Branding

The distinctive rumble of a Harley Davidson® engine. The four simple musical bleeps that mean "Intel® Inside." Three notes that translate to "N-B-C." The Nokia® ringtone. The brief, soaring, optimistic tune that greets you every time you boot up Windows®. Never underestimate the power of sound to invoke recognition and memory. Through imagery transfer, brief arrangements of notes can take on the same power as a visual logo. They can become a sonic brand—a distinctive sound that calls a company's name to mind every time it's heard.

Remember the 1980s series "The Dukes of Hazzard"? The Duke boys' car horn was unique—it played a very specific tune. To this day, any customized auto horn that plays "Dixie" brings to mind The General Lee—through a powerful sonic brand.

The upshot is, just a short snippet of your jingle can be enough to keep you at the forefront of your target customer's mind.

How To Ensure Imagery Transfer

- **Start with the music.** A memorable, well-crafted, professional-sounding jingle is the most critical piece of a campaign that's designed to leverage imagery transfer. Without a high-quality jingle that people actually like, the rest of the campaign will quite literally fall apart. Imagery transfer depends on a chain of events in the human brain, and they all start with the ear.

- **Build your television ads on your jingle**—not the other way around. Resist the urge to let your video producer "run with" the creative process and slap your jingle over the top of the finished product. The storyboarding process should carefully match up key points in your jingle copy with powerful, memorable, favorable visual images.

- **Establish strong visual ties between lyrics and imagery.** When your company's name is sung, feature the logo. If your jingle lyrics mention family, match up that portion of the jingle with an image of a happy family. And so on. You can't get too literal.

- **Make sure the quality levels of sound and visuals are equivalent.** In other words, don't marry a polished, professional jingle with video production that looks like Uncle Ned shot it with two flashlights on a camcorder. If you want people to remember visual elements when they hear your radio jingle, it pays to make those visuals *as appealing as possible.*

- **Repeat the visuals in eye-oriented media.** Once the radio and television portions of the ad are finished, you can count on image transference to tickle recall when your target audience sees the same logo on a billboard, the side of your building, or in a print ad announcing all the details of a special sale.

CHAPTER 11: THE BIG CHALLENGE

When you run a business that relies primarily on local buyers, your first challenge is to understand why and *how consumers choose to buy* from one business rather than another. You can only create effective advertising and marketing outreach if you understand the *W*'s:

1. Who are your customers?

2. What do they want?

3. Why do they want it?

4. When do they want it?

5. Where will they look for it?

The Sound Of Selling: AIDA

To understand the power of jingles, it helps to understand how advertising and selling work.

Your spots should sing AIDA, and we don't mean the Verdi opera.

A = Attention

I = Interest

D = Desire

A = Action

AIDA is a powerful 4-step buying cycle formula that can be applied to radio and television campaigns. Professors and academic types who study and write about marketing contend that every consumer passes through several steps in their buying cycle, and AIDA can help to influence their decisions.

This famous model was developed by Lavidge and Steiner in 1961, later to be dubbed the *AIDA: Hierarchy of Effects Model* by Palda in 1966. This approach involves the hierarchy of effects: awareness, knowledge, liking, preference, conviction and finally purchase, in that order. Here is a quick rundown of how they work in concert. More on each phase of the buy cycle is coming up.

A = Attention: Advertisements need to catch your consumers' attention. A great ad must excite prospective customers when they hear it. The jingle is the perfect place to choose and emphasize one great benefit—a single overarching differentiator. In lots of ways, jingles are the ultimate attention-getters because they follow the old acronym KISS—Keep It Short and Simple (or the rude version, Keep it Simple, Stupid).

I = Interest: Now that you've got their attention, you need to generate real interest. Remember, customers buy benefits, not features—that means they buy the sizzle, not the steak, and the sexy image of a Camaro, not an engine and tires. In broadcast advertising, you create interest by emotionally selling potential customers on multiple benefits that can enhance their life.

D = Desire: Once advertising has captured audience attention and interest, *then* you can tailor the message to create desire, making your offer irresistible. Include heaps of free bonuses in your radio and television spots. Include an extraordinary guarantee. Build urgency into every offer.

A = Action. Last, but most important, your radio and television spots must have a *call to action*. Tell your potential customers what you want them to do. Even if you have captured their attention, overwhelmed them with benefits and created an undeniable desire, you must still ask them to buy.

There you have it. Compare the AIDA formula against every radio and television ad you are currently using and against every future spot you create. While creating memorable advertising takes time in the beginning, you will find yourself creating better and better campaigns fueled by the power of jingles.

Attention, Shoppers...

AIDA's first "A"—Attention—is the most critical component of effective broadcast advertising. Get their attention in the first few seconds and there's a decent chance they'll listen to your whole message. Lose their attention with wishy-washy, dull, drab, sounds-like-everybody-else ads, and you've just wasted your ad budget. You'll never move them through Interest to Desire and Action if you don't succeed at Attention.

As blocks of ads get longer, it's not unusual for your message to be sandwiched in the middle of five to fifteen other ads. The first critical few seconds of an effective broadcast ad needs to grab people by the collar and focus their awareness on what's coming.

Instant identification is increasingly a best practice in advertising. You may have noticed that advertisers use a variety of devices to indicate whose message this is—or at least what it's going to be about—right up front. One increasingly common tactic to instantly identify an advertiser is the **auditory mnemonic**—a distinctive sound that is exclusively associated with one company and helps consumers remember their name. Over time, consistency and repetition create an audio "brand" that's priceless.

Well written music lends itself to instantaneous recognition. The first chords of a song can literally transport you through time, sending you back to childhood, or grammar school, or high school; think of the opening chords of "Stairway to Heaven," or "California Girls," or "Yesterday."

Especially now, in an era when ad time is more expensive than ever (and available slots fewer and fewer), customers appreciate knowing an advertiser's identity earlier, rather than later. When you're purchasing :30 and :15 second ads rather than :60s, it's obviously a good idea to make those seconds count.

- For more than four decades, NBC has used a distinctive series of three chime tones to identify itself.

- Intel uses four recognizable notes behind its "Intel Inside" logo.

- When you boot up your Microsoft® Windows® computer, you hear a brief swell of music that belongs only to the software giant.

- Rice-a-Roni built up a very recognizable auditory brand with the ringing of cable car bells.

- The first global McDonald's campaign, introduced in 2003, uses a brief recognizable musical intro before any actual lyrics are sung— "Ba da ba-ba-ba…I'm Lovin' It!"

Here are a couple of other attention-getting tricks that can make your first two seconds sing:

Sound Effects. Selling beer, soda, or something else that fizzes? Consider the sound of a can opening. Fresh veggies the calling card at your gourmet hideaway? The crunchy sound of teeth meeting celery might be the way to get people to associate "fresh" with you. Selling security products or insurance? Nothing will prick up ears like the sound of a police or ambulance siren. Automotive repairs your specialty? It might be a cliché, but the smooth revving of a well-tuned engine can put your target customers in gear to hear about this week's specials. Carefully chosen and used consistently, sound effects that open a broadcast ad can really get people ready to hear your sales message.

Musical Fanfare. For years, big brands like Budweiser, McDonalds, and State Farm have used high-quality musical advertising campaigns. Then, after consumers heard "When you say Budweiser, You've said it all" or "We do it all for you" enough times, the lyrics were unnecessary. Just the sound of the opening musical signature is enough to for consumers to know who's sponsoring the upcoming message. Local advertisers with distinctive musical campaigns do well when they learn from the "big guys."

Early in your broadcast advertising campaign, use a "donut" cut of a customized jingle (see page 105). Have the company name sung first, before anything else. Eventually, just like the big national advertisers, your listeners will associate your name with the music. Eventually, the music itself will say "you," and you can move to just a "sing-out"—or perhaps no lyrics at all. The music itself will have gotten Attention, and you'll still have almost a full :30 or :60 to build Interest, Desire, and Action.

Chapter 12: Understanding Buyer Behavior

Almost without exception, being in business is a challenge because very few people wake up each morning with a burning desire to purchase your goods or services. They buy from you only when they perceive a *need* for what you sell.

Every purchase goes through either a short or long Buy Cycle. In general, the higher the pricetag, urgency or importance of the purchase, the longer the cycle will be. (In other words, it takes very little time to go through these five steps when you're buying a candy bar; it takes much longer to go through them when you're shopping for your next car.)

The Buy Cycle's Five Steps

1. Problem Recognition

2. Information Search

3. Awareness of Options

4. Option Evaluation

5. Post-Purchase Behavior

The next five chapters will walk you through each phase and help you to think about how you can influence buyer behavior in some of these phases. Keep AIDA in mind as you go; think of the formula as training wheels for consumers on their buy-cycles. Your broadcast advertising can get attention, stir interest, inflame desire, and drive people to action.

CHAPTER 13: PROBLEM RECOGNITION

The most fundamental basis of consumer buying is awareness of a need.

It's a basic truth, but it bears saying: Unless somebody has a need *and* knows it, *you don't have a prospective customer.*

Some advertising works remind customers they have a problem. Every Autumn, for example, automotive repair shops remind consumers that it's time to check their batteries and get the family ride ready for cold weather.

Some advertising makes people *believe* they have a problem, even if they may not have recognized it before. In recent years, ads for prescription drugs have been allowed on broadcast media. Almost every drug ad attempts to "help" consumers realize they have a problem. Heartburn used to be just plain old heartburn; now it's Acid Reflux Disease.

Often, ads that are aimed at stirring consumers to recognize a problem use questions. Do you have acne? Itchy skin? A headache? Toenail fungus? Indigestion? Depression? Sexual dysfunction? Could it be something worse? Have you seen your doctor? Don't you need a new prescription for SOMETHING? Tired of cleaning the house? Worried that your mutual fund load is unbalanced? Does your chewing gum lose its flavor?

Not surprisingly, some great advertising slogans (and jingles) throughout the years have been questions that are aimed straight at the Problem Recognition phase of consumer buying behavior.

- Have you driven a Ford® lately?

- Is two months' salary too much to spend on something that lasts forever? (DeBeers®)

- What would you do for a Klondike® Bar?

DeBeers had such success with their "two months' salary" campaign, it's now generally accepted practice in North America for a male suitor to spend that much on an engagement ring. Talk about an advertising campaign that created a true, pressing sense of a problem!

Pepsi's Great Breakthrough

Consider the granddaddy of all radio jingles, the Pepsi-Cola spot of 1939.

In 1931, Pepsi went bankrupt for the second time, but the new owner, Roy Megargel, would hit upon an idea that would finally give Coca-Cola some competition. In 1934, he marketed Pepsi in a 12-ounce bottle for a nickel. At the time, Coca-Cola was sold in a 6-ounce bottle for ten cents. Voila! Profits for Pepsi.

Pepsi racked up another first by airing the first national radio jingle in 1939. Like some other jingles through the years, it became so popular that it was played in jukeboxes and became a hit record.

Jingle Break

Pepsi-Cola hits the spot.
12 full ounces, that's a lot!
Twice as much for a nickel, too.
Pepsi-Cola is the drink for you!

In 1949, that little number played 296,426 times on 469 radio stations—not counting jukebox play, where it was also a favorite.

According to *Advertising Age* magazine, the Pepsi jingle embedded itself not so much in the nation's psyche as in its very nerve endings, like the Pledge of Allegiance.

Our Own Jingle: Sold In Sixty Seconds

When we sat down and talked about the "Sold in Sixty Seconds" concept, we realized this was a great opportunity to demonstrate what we're talking about in this book. So we set about writing a jingle about jingles.

The concept was simple. Still, we made a lot of decisions. What kind of music would work best with a message about jingles? Classical? Nah. Blues? Maybe, but we aren't a bluesy kind of company. We have fun with our clients, and we wanted a piece of music that would capture that sense of fun.

We came up with an original piece of music that would showcase the phrase "Sold In Sixty Seconds" and we wrapped that around lines that show how nerve-wracking it can be to buy broadcast advertising. We wanted people to hear a jingle that made them smile, but also made them understand how much easier it is to remember a phrase when it's set to music. So we kept the lyrics simple. We added a bit of humor, and we hammered home the core message.

When you listen to the jingle, think about how it makes you feel—do you get the idea that creating a jingle is a fun experience? Finally, when it's over, ask yourself, "What was that tag line again?" You'll probably hum it to yourself!

One, Two Three…
Sold in Sixty Seconds, Sold in Sixty Seconds
You only got a minute
The clock is running out of time
(only got a minute, only got a minute)
The message gotta catch on fire
It's getting down to the wire

The copy is slick
But will anything stick?
Or maybe it's time to retire….
(Shoulda listened to my mother…coulda been a lawyer!)

Down to half a minute
The sweat's pouring down your face
But if you never, ever want to regret it

Make it music — They'll never forget it
Burn your brand into their brain

Sold in 60 seconds
Sold in 60 seconds
Sold in 60 seconds…

DONE!

CHAPTER 14: INFORMATION SEARCH

Once a potential buyer recognizes that they have a problem and a specific need for the kind of product or service you sell, they're through the first A in AIDA. They've moved onto Interest. They're ready to begin looking for ways to solve their problem.

Researchers and professors of marketing have taken the trouble to map what happens in a consumer's mind as they get ready to buy.

Internal information search happens when the only place the potential buyer looks for answers is his or her own memory. The questions he or she asks are: *How can I solve this problem? Where can I get what I need?*

Internal information searches are generally restricted to low-cost, low-importance or hard-to-differentiate purchases. If you're hungry for a candy bar, chances are high that you're not going to fire up the Internet and start comparing ingredients. What's already in your head is plenty of information for your decision.

Internal searches may also be used when the purchase is very important, but there's not a lot of time to spend looking for the best price or even the best brand.

Say, for another example, the in-laws are arriving from Toledo tomorrow. Mr. and Mrs. Newlyweds don't have a spare bed. If you run the local mattress store, you want the *first place* they think of to be… *your place.* You want to pop up in their internal information search.

Bottom line: If your business isn't somewhere in the top three when your potential customers are flipping through their mental Rolodex, you're in trouble. An ad campaign that gets you into a consumer's mind is the only way to make sure you're on the short list.

An **external information search**, on the other hand, is longer and more complicated. These tend to take a while longer—from hours to months, depending on the size of the purchase. Something new happens in an external search, as well: The potential buyer looks to his or her environment to help gather information and create a short list of ways to solve the problem.

That means potential buyer actively consult newspapers, radio, television, magazines, style or buyer's guides, friends, family—in other words, they seek out sources of information that are not already in memory.

Not surprisingly, for many local advertisers, the best selling opportunities are when the buy cycle is short and the information search is internal. This is the reason why corner convenience markets always have milk and lunch meat on hand in addition to gasoline and motor oil. These business owners know that tired, busy people who are getting gas before or after work will often do a quick internal information search while they wash the windshield and opt to stock up on essential fridge items at the same place, rather than going to the grocery store across town.

Jingles that burn a brand into your brain make the internal information search easier for a buyer. Therefore, jingles make it more likely that the next time somebody has a need, they'll think of you.

Quick! Think of a couple of brands of hot dogs.

```
┌────────────────────────────────────────────────────┐
│  Armour® Hot dogs                                    │
│                                                      │
│            Hot dogs, Armour hot dogs                 │
│    What kinds of kids love Armour hot dogs?          │
│              Fat kids, skinny kids                   │
│            Kids who climb on rocks                   │
│             Tough kids, sissy kids                   │
│           Even kids with chicken pox                 │
│                 Love hot dogs                        │
│                Armour hot dogs                       │
│           The dogs kids love to bite!                │
│                                                      │
└────────────────────────────────────────────────────┘


┌────────────────────────────────────────────────────┐
│  Oscar Meyer®                                        │
│                                                      │
│       Oh I wish I were an Oscar Meyer                │
│                    Weiner                            │
│        That is what I'd truly like to be             │
│     For if I were an Oscar Meyer Weiner              │
│      Everyone would be in love with me               │
│                                                      │
└────────────────────────────────────────────────────┘
```

Did you remember either of these brands? If you did, chances are the jingles themselves burned the brand into your brain in the 1970s.

Now that's *long-term* brand reinforcement!

Chapter 15: The Buyer's Options

As consumers move from Interest to Desire in the consumer opera called AIDA, they begin to weigh their options.

Marketing and advertising professionals have done mountains of research into this phase of the consumer buy cycle. Here are a few more concepts that you may find useful.

Awareness set

In an internal search, the "awareness set" is the group of companies, stores, brands or products that the potential buyer knows exist. They might not remember them without prompting, though. Researchers typically ask "Are you aware of these brands?" and then list them when they're interviewing to find awareness sets in market research.

Evoked set

The "evoked set" is a shorter list: They're the *first* companies, stores, brands or products that come to mind in a particular situation. Scholars who study marketing and advertising often call this phenomenon "top of mind awareness;" it's also been described as "rapid recall." A market researcher would be asking for an evoked set if she asked, "When I say bathroom tissue, what brands do you think of right off the top of your head?"

Consideration set

The "consideration" set is part of the evoked set. This group of options includes brands that are acceptable for further consideration. There are also two less desirable (for the seller) subsets of the Evoked Set.

Inert set

The inert set is made up of options about which the buyer is indifferent. It's highly unlikely that the purchase will happen at a member of the inert set, *unless* the buy cycle is long and the external information search uncovers very convincing evidence in favor of buying one of the inert set brands. If a car buyer, for example, has never set foot on three of the five auto dealerships in town, but has purchased her last six vehicles from two dealerships, then the three she's never visited are the inert set. She won't break her habit of shopping the other two dealerships *unless* the three inert dealers offer some sort of incentive she couldn't get through her usual seller.

Inept set

The inept set includes options that are, for one reason or another, considered unacceptable. These are usually discarded almost immediately: *No, I hate Joe's Pizza; he doesn't use enough sauce. No, I won't go to Crunchy's Drugstore, because the guy at the counter there was rude to me in 1987 and I'll never shop there again. No, I wouldn't drive an imported car if you held a nail gun to my head.*

Your aim, as a local advertiser, is to be in all three GOOD groups: The Awareness Set, the Evoked Set and the Consideration Set.

In plain English, you want to be among the top few businesses of your kind that people remember when they need *your* kind of product or services and ask themselves questions like...

- *Where can I get some antacid?*
- *Where can I get some of that toenail fungus stuff?*
- *How can I feed the kids quickly tonight?*

In the case of the "Sold in Sixty Seconds" jingle, the question is, "How can I get the most bang for my buck when I advertise?"

To sum up, you arouse Interest and create Desire when you:

- Use SHORT, SIMPLE messages. CLARITY is critical.

- Detail additional benefits. Prospects want to know "what can you do for me?"

- Make sure your spot is easy to understand.

Here are some classic jingles that arouse interest in information features and benefits.

Almond Joy®

Sometimes you feel like a nut
Sometimes you don't
Almond Joy's got nuts
Mounds don't
Almond Joy's got real milk chocolate
Coconut and crunchy nuts too
Mounds' got deep dark chocolate
And chewy coconut (oooh)
Sometimes you feel like a nut
Sometimes you don't!

Big Red® Gum

So kiss a little longer
hold hands a little longer
hold tight a little longer
Longer with Big Red
That Big Red freshness lasts right through it
Your fresh breath goes on and on
while you chew it
Say goodbye a little longer
make it last a little longer
Give your breath long lasting freshness
with Big Red

Crackerjack®

Candy-coated popcorn,
peanuts, and a prize,
that's what you get
in Crackerjack

Spaghettios®

The neat new spaghetti
you can eat with a spoon
Uh, oh, spaghettios
Neat round spaghetti
that will stay on your spoon
Uh, oh, spaghettios

Bosco®

I love Bosco, it's rich and chocolate-y
Chocolate-flavored Bosco
is mighty good for me
Mama puts it in my milk for extra energy
Bosco gives me iron and sunshine
Vitamin D
Oh, I love Bosco
that's the drink for me

CHAPTER 16: EVALUATION OF ALTERNATIVES

Once a buyer knows there's a problem and there are ways to fix it, she or he has to get down to the actual brass tacks—deciding which alternative to choose.

Again, not surprisingly, in low-risk decision-making, this step is simple.

There's not a lot of risk in deciding which candy bar to pick up at the convenience store. *Do I want a Kit Kat® or a Hershey® Bar?* The decision criteria will probably be as simple as, "Do I want a pure chocolate fix or am I in the mood for crunch?"

In higher risk buying situations, though, when there's a lot of money, prestige or ego on the line, evaluation of options starts to get longer and more complicated, and you, as a local business, must give consumers reasons to choose you rather than the huge national chains.

Consider the question, *Where should I buy my girlfriend an engagement ring?*

Here are some options.

- SuperMegaMart

- Mom & Pop's Jewels

- Over the Internet at a discount site

- Tiffany's

- Jake's Pawnshop

There are arguments that could be made for all five points of purchase, depending on the young Groom-To-Be's priorities.

If you're Mom & Pop's Jewels, your ads need to explain the reasons he should come to you. Chances are, the reasons will have something to do with tradition, service, friendliness and hometown values. If the groom is a traditional romantic, then an ad like that will speak to him and chances are good he'll walk into your store.

If you're Jake's Pawnshop, on the other hand, your ads will be a little different. The kind of young man who'd pick up an engagement ring at a pawnshop (not that there's anything wrong with that…) is probably a little rebellious, short on cash and not traditional in the least. Still, he's out there and he's proposing to a young lady. Jake's job is to put together an ad campaign that will speak to those young men and make them feel like it's OK—maybe even *cool*—to defy convention and pick up the rock at the same place he shops for used guitars and tools.

Both Jake and Mom & Pop have stories to tell and should be using the power and leverage of local advertising to tell their stories.

Then there's another consideration: To compete effectively with Tiffany's and SuperMegaMart, both of which have HUGE advertising budgets and high-quality ads. Jake and Mom & Pop must sound like *different but equivalent* options. If Mom & Pop's broadcast advertising ends up sounding corny or amateurish, it may actually be worse for business, because a low-quality ad transfers the image of low quality to their business itself.

A Study of Audience Impressions With Jingles

According to Poole-Adamson Research Consultants Ltd., one of the better bets for improving your advertising in radio is to use a jingle. The reason is that the *audience gets more involved* when the message is musical. Ads that only use the spoken word tend to be tuned out or instantly forgotten. You get more durability (the audience remembers the ad) and far better brand delivery (the audience remembers *you*) when there's a business-specific jingle in an ad. See the chart that follows for some solid, empirical evidence. This information comes from Poole-Adamson Research Consultants, Ltd.

Type of Audience Response	With or Without Jingles	
	With	*Without*
Involvement	51	46
Personal Appeal	57	51
Durability	59	52
Product Substantiveness	52	53
Brand Presence	87	62
Basic Purchase Conviction	40	38

The researchers make a distinction between ads that incorporate jingles, those whose copy is merely sung and those that employ music for ambiance or mere effect. These latter types behave quite differently than the "jingle" types.

To subscribe to their newsletter, send an e-mail message to Terry Poole (tpoole@interlog.com) at Poole-Adamson Research Consultants Ltd. with the word "subscribe" in the subject line.

Chapter 17: Purchase Decision

The final act of AIDA is short. Decision and Action usually go hand in hand—like peanut butter and jelly or bacon and eggs.

When you advertise, you shouldn't assume that prospects know what to do. Tell them what ACTION to take.

- Should they visit your store?

- See your Web site for more information?

- Place an order by phone?

From a buying cycle standpoint, sometimes your goal is to move them closer to a decision (Come test drive a car!). Other times, you'll want consumers to make a buying decision on the spot (*Come in today and get three sets of earrings for the price of two!*). Whichever your goal, your spots should ask them to take action. Tell them to *do something* once the ad is over.

To make it easy for prospects, you might want to:

- **Provide your Web site address.** This makes it easy to respond to offers, request more information, ask you a question and more.

- **Mention your phone number and street address.** Some businesses have actually used music, rhyme and rhythm to teach phone numbers and addresses to their audiences. Starting in the 1970s, a Chicago carpeting company, Empire, has ended each of its television and radio ads with a group singing their phone number: *Five Eight Eight, Two Three Hundred, Empire.* There's also *Hudson Two Three Seven Hundred.* And the children's show *Zoom* made sure that its fans could always find them. All these years later, a good number of thirtysomething Americans can sing along to *Zoom, Z double-O M, Box Three Five Oh, Boston Mass, Ooooh, Two One, Three Fooouur… Send it to Zoom!*

- Give them an **incentive to respond NOW.** Offer them a premium for responding by a certain date or a discount for being among the first 100 people who visit the store, take a test-drive or call for more information.

CHAPTER 18: POST-PURCHASE BEHAVIOR

If you've ever gotten home in your brand new car and then developed a nagging sense of doubt over the following few days about whether you've made a horrible mistake… you know all about the last step in the consumer buy cycle.

Once a buying decision is made, the purchase isn't over. There's also a period after the purchase when the consumer continues to think about whether he or she received good value for the investment. The more important, risky or pricey the purchase was, the longer this evaluation will last.

"Buyer's Remorse" is one end of the post-purchase behavior spectrum. Enormous satisfaction is the other.

Local market advertisers often have the opportunity to make or break their businesses with personal service and post-sale attention that go well beyond what buyers would receive at SuperMegaMart.

Assuming you take good care of your customers, they'll spread the word. And that means the next time you play AIDA with them (and their families and friends who have now heard good things about you), the cycle can start all over again.

☑ A Checklist: Where in the Customer Buy Cycle Could Your Advertising Work Better To Get More Customers?

	Problem Awareness: Many of my potential customers don't even know they need what I sell or they don't understand why they need it. I need to get them to understand why they should come see me.
	Information Search: Many of my customers aren't even aware I exist yet. I need to work harder to make sure I'm always a part of their Awareness, Evoked and Consideration set. I need to get into their memory!
	Alternatives Evaluation: I think most of my potential buyers know we exist, but I need to make it clear why they should choose *my* goods or services over the competition's.
	Post-Purchase Behavior: I need to remind all of my satisfied customers why they had such a great experience so they'll come back to me next time they need what I sell, *and* tell all their friends and neighbors about how much better I am than SuperMegaMart.

Armed with this checklist, you're geared up for the challenge of creating an advertising campaign that will be able to work on all of the phases of the consumer buy cycle. You also have a starting point for your jingle development.

Our own jingle, "Sold in Sixty Seconds," focuses on the awareness and information search portions of the buy cycle. Most broadcast advertisers know there's such a thing as a jingle, but they may not immediately link it to their own needs. With a jingle that speaks directly to advertisers, we aim to burn our brand into their brains.

Chapter 19: A Jingle That's Stood The Test Of Time

In May of 2004, Roto-Rooter® celebrated half a century of singing "Call Roto-Rooter, that's the name, and away go troubles down the drain." (Those two simple lines contain both a statement of benefit and a call to action; pretty good use of just a few seconds, wouldn't you say?)

Roto-Rooter was established in 1935 and today is the largest provider of plumbing and drain cleaning services in the United States and Canada. The company operates businesses in more than 100 company-owned territories and more than 500 franchise territories, serving approximately 90 percent of the U.S. population.

The plumbing company's jingle anniversary begs the question: Are jingles making a comeback? Jingles became popular on the radio when companies like Brylcreem and Campbell's Soup developed their catchy tunes like "a little dab'll do ya" (1946) and "Mmm, Mmm, Good" (1931). However, as consumers got more skeptical and advertising began to clutter the airwaves, some advertisers moved away from them or revised them musically to mimic current hit tunes. Roto-Rooter is one of the only companies to leave its jingle untouched for this long.

In the competitive marketplace, industries from automotive to fast food constantly try fresh ways to reach the American consumer. As a result, the advertising jingle has ridden a roller-coaster ride no different than that of a musical genre. Some jingles created over the years have fallen on deaf ears, while others have stood the test of time.

According to a recent survey of 1,000 Americans, Wrigley's "double your pleasure, double your fun," Roto-Rooter's "...and away go troubles down the drain," and GM's "see the USA in your Chevrolet" ranked as the top three most familiar jingles of yesteryear.

In particular, Americans born between 1950 and 1969 remember "Roto-Rooter, that's the name... and away go troubles down the drain." Captain Stubby and the Buccaneers first performed the jingle in 1954 on WLS Radio in Chicago. Since that time the Roto-Rooter jingle has been featured in countless advertisements for the company and is now a bona fide piece of Americana.

"While I participated in several other musical productions over the years, the Roto-Rooter jingle is forever in my heart," said Tom Fouts, 84, also known as the Captain. "Recording such an unforgettable piece of American history is an experience that I will always treasure."

Captain Stubby's legacy is far from forgotten. Interestingly, three of four Americans surveyed remember the Captain's contribution to this musical advertising vehicle. According to Spencer Lee, CEO for Roto-Rooter, the jingle has had a significant effect on business over the years.

"Roto-Rooter can attribute much of its long-standing reputation to the appeal of its 50-year-old jingle," says Lee. "The fact that people can still sing the tune today shows just how linked it has become to our brand and our popularity with homeowners."

So, will Coke teach "the world to sing" again? Will Oscar Mayer's bologna continue to have a first name? Whether or not jingles find their way into pop culture as widely as they did years ago, one thing is certain—an undeniable connection exists between music and effective advertising. The popularity and nostalgia of advertising jingles represent ways in which music continues to influence virtually every aspect of our lives.

Roto-Rooter began celebrating the jingle's 50th anniversary in May 2004. While the jingle has always appeared in Roto-Rooter radio, TV spots and Yellow Page ads, the company has added the famous musical scroll to its billboard and print advertising campaigns.

CHAPTER 20: THE MUSIC

The Music

There are as many musical styles as there are tastes. The range of choices may seem overwhelming at the outset, but the good news is, any good jingle producer should be able to come up with music you love as the foundation for your jingle.

Style

The next few chapters will describe the most popular musical styles and help you to understand what kinds of businesses might choose each kind of music. Every piece of music (just the music, not the words) has several elements.

Tempo

The tempo of a piece of music is its speed. Is it slow? Is it fast? Is it somewhere in between? Fast music is called "up-tempo" in the music production business. Slow music is "down-tempo." Does the tempo complement the style? (If you play a march too fast, you end up with a run... fine if you're looking for a humorous effect, but not so much if you're advertising something serious.)

Rhythm

Rhythm is the arrangement of the beats in a song. Usually drums will form the backbone of a song's rhythm, but sometimes other instruments (like bass or even a tuba) can do the same. The following are a couple of patterns of rhythm. The music's rhythm determines how the lyrics must be composed to sound good.

Oom-pah pah, Ooom-pah pah
Rat-a-tat-tat
Boom boom WHACK! Boom boom WHACK!
Da Da Dum, Da Da Dum, Da Da Dum-Dum-Dum
Boom, Boom, acka-lacka-lacka boom

Melody

Simply put, a melody is the arrangement of notes that are sung in a vocal piece. The melody is the part of a jingle that forces the subconscious to "sing along" even when the lyrics aren't there in the recording. (Anybody who's ever heard an instrumental rendition of the Beatles' "Yesterday" knows how impossible it is not to start warbling "love was such an easy game to play.") The power of melody is what will have customers in your town humming your tune—even after the commercial is over.

Some forms of music, like soft rock and traditional country, tend to focus almost exclusively on the melody, while other forms like classical weave together more than just one set of notes to create harmonies and counterpoints. It's even possible to have music without melody—listen to some hip-hop or rap and you'll see what we mean.

CHAPTER 21: ANTHEMS

As you skim the next few chapters, think about the radio ads you've liked over the years—both local and national. Do you tend to like Pop more than anything else? Country? Do you respond to the soaring emotion of Anthems? Or do you think the mellow, laid-back strains of Country will fit your unique message and business?

We present these genres for your consideration along with a few of the kinds of businesses that have used them through the years. While almost any business can "get away" with almost any kind of music, some business/music partnerships are more natural, and these chapters should help you to sort out the top few possibilities for your own, unique music.

Music in the Anthem category sounds emotional, hopeful and robust. You hear an anthem and your chest swells just a little. You can't help it. It sounds like the kind of music you hear at an outdoor arena concert when all those lighters fire up. A really good anthem can actually bring a tear to your eye!

Anthems are a great sound for businesses that are looking for an image that is:

Traditional	Optimistic
Prosperous	Inspiring
Heroic	Patriotic
Larger-than-life	Proud

Kinds of Businesses That Use Anthem Music

- Banks or financial institutions
- Hospitals
- Home maintenance and repair services that work around the clock (heating, plumbing, air conditioning)
- Political candidates and initiatives
- Charities and nonprofit organizations

CHAPTER 22: SWING

Now you're cooking. Swing music is all the rage, Daddy-O!

From the great swing bands of yesteryear like Benny Goodman to the Brian Setzer Orchestra today, you know swing is music that has the power to make you want to move. It's zesty, energetic, bouncy, get-up-on-the-dance-floor, go-crazy-in-a-wholesome-way music. With horns galore and up-tempo catchiness, it's a great sound that evokes the era of USO shows and sheer physical fun.

Swing creates a wonderful bed of music for businesses that are looking for an image that is:

Fun	Nostalgic
Bold	Happy
Energetic	Uninhibited

Kinds of Businesses That Choose Swing Music

- Auto dealers and service/repair facilities
- Financial institutions like mortgage companies and savings-and-loans
- Insurance and real estate agencies
- Family restaurants
- Clubs and entertainment venues

CHAPTER 23: BIG BAND

Big Band is the comforting sound of The Good Old Days: Kids on bicycles, sunshine, lemonade stands, warm days, innocent sock hops and traditional American values.

Big Band is the musical equivalent of a Norman Rockwell painting— happy, reassuring, friendly, evocative of the simpler days when everybody lived in a golden haze of small-town bliss.

Even if they never did.

Big Band is a great sound for businesses that are looking for an image that is:

Classic	Carefree
Positive	Reminiscent
Dignified	Warm
Comfortable	Homey

Kinds of Businesses That Choose Big Band Music

- Hometown furniture or hardware store
- Hotels and resorts
- Real estate developments or home subdivisions
- Retirement communities
- "Golden Years" products and services
- RV dealerships

CHAPTER 24: BLUES

A blues-y jingle is a memorable jingle. Why? Blues is a style of music that lends itself to repetition, which works a message into a listener's head almost immediately.

Traditional blues songs use a simple chord structure and repetitive words that make it easy to sing along from the first time you hear a song. Usually, blues lyrics repeat the same line twice, creating tension in the listener, then finish off with a bang.

You ain't nothing but a hound dog crying all the time
You ain't nothing but a hound dog crying all the time
Well you ain't never caught a rabbit and you ain't no friend of mine

A bluesy jingle could be right for businesses that are:

Down-home	Informal
Welcoming	Lively
Entertaining	Friendly

Kinds of Businesses That Choose Blues Music

- Restaurant Bar and Grill
- Auto dealers, especially trucks and SUVs
- Auto repair shops
- Video stores
- Malls and shopping centers
- Casinos

CHAPTER 25: CLASSICAL

Classical music is full of strings, horns and so on. It's the most formal of the musical styles and it's usually used when the potential buyer is somebody who might actually go to an opera or the theatre or is throwing a formal event where people will get dressed up. Think wedding flowers.

Classical music is great for businesses that are:

Luxurious	Exclusive
Related to beauty	Extravagant
Dignified	Intellectual
Sophisticated	Elegant

Kinds of Businesses That Choose Classical Music

- Florists, caterers and photographers
- Luxury auto dealerships
- Clothing or gift boutiques
- Funeral homes
- Jewelers
- Art dealers

CHAPTER 26: TRADITIONAL COUNTRY

Hank Williams. Johnny Cash. George Jones. Tammy Wynette. Loretta Lynn. When the music sounds like it ought to be about honkytonks, good-timing, old dogs, cigarettes and watermelon wine, you're in Traditional Country territory.

Traditional Country is slide guitars, banjos, steel guitars, fiddles, harmonicas and tambourines. Good, solid, all-American music for good, solid, all-American businesses.

Patriotic	Family-oriented
Friendly	Warm
Trustworthy	Dependable
Traditional	Heartfelt

Kinds of Businesses That Choose Traditional Country Music

- Truck, RV and camper dealerships
- Sport vehicle dealerships
- Outdoor and sporting goods stores
- Family restaurants
- Local recreation venues
- Lumber and building supply

CHAPTER 27: HOT COUNTRY

Tim McGraw, Garth Brooks, Reba McEntire, Martina McBride, Brooks & Dunn. It's a combination of country and rock-and-roll, all revved up. It's grab-your-partner-and-go-line-dancing music.

Hot Country is good for building an image that's:

Fun	Assertive
Energetic	Gritty
Edgy	Sexy
Playful	Strong

Kinds of Businesses That Choose Hot Country Music

- Truck or sport vehicle dealers
- Motorcycle and motorsport dealerships
- Outdoor sporting equipment
- Lube/oil/filter facilities
- Casinos
- Hospitality and entertainment businesses
- Theme restaurants
- Sports bars

CHAPTER 28: JAZZ

Doesn't matter if it's Smooth, New Orleans or Traditional, Jazz is a form of music that's entirely American. Horns are practically mandatory, and even when it's improvised, Jazz usually has a very put-together sound that's slick, polished and soothing.

It's a great music choice for companies that want to reinforce an image that's:

Sophisticated	Elegant
Professional	Classy
Experienced	Trustworthy
High Quality	Exclusive

Kinds of Businesses That Choose Jazz Music

- Upscale auto dealers
- Eye-care, physicians or healthcare
- Day spas and beauty salons
- Home design, builders and developments
- Retail clothing or gifts
- Florists
- Jewelers

CHAPTER 29: MOTOWN

The Supremes, Stevie Wonder, Smokey Robinson, The Temptations. It's a throwback to earlier eras.

Passionate	Positive
Familiar	Feel-good
Happy	Friendly
Groovy	Soulful

Kinds of Businesses That Choose Motown Music

- Banks and credit unions
- Malls and shopping centers
- Casinos and entertainment businesses
- New and Used Auto Dealers, sedans, family cars
- Clothing stores
- Restaurants
- Community Groups
- Mattress Shops

CHAPTER 30: NOVELTY

Novelty music is just plain silly. It makes you laugh and puts a smile on your face, but beware: it's not for the faint of heart. Novelty music is one of the quickest to wear out its welcome. So, if you're planning on flooding the airwaves, make sure you're willing to occasionally annoy people in exchange for getting in their memory and staying there—whether they like it or not, they're going to sing along.

The image that grows from a Novelty musical background is:

Quirky	Humorous
Happy-go-lucky	Playful
Light	Goofy
Childlike	Silly

Kinds of Businesses That Choose Novelty Music

- Family restaurants and fun centers
- Children's toy or clothing stores
- Hard-to-differentiate services like appliance repair
- Multiplexes
- County fairs, expos and special events
- Yogurt, ice cream and dessert shops
- Hobby stores

CHAPTER 31: OLDIES ROCK

Elvis, The Beatles, Chuck Berry, Bill Haley, Buddy Holly, Beach Boys. It was the music that shaped the Baby Boom generation and now that those Boomers make up the largest consuming age group, Oldies get a good workout in the world of jingles.

Oldies rock is valued for its ability to hearken back to the days of Dad's '57 Chevy, Mom's surfer girl summers and Uncle Ted's paper route. Oldies are a good bet if you want an image for your business that's:

Warm	Happy
Nostalgic	Genuine
Fun	Honest
Peppy	Simple

Kinds of Businesses That Choose Oldies Music

- Diners and Restaurants
- Plumbing, Heating, Air Conditioning
- American Car Dealerships, sportscars
- Pools and Spas
- Printing and Graphics
- Clothing
- Businesses that cater to Baby-boomers

CHAPTER 32: POP

Celine Dion, Madonna, Matchbox Twenty, Britney Spears, Dave Matthews, Prince, Elton John, Backstreet Boys, Justin Timberlake. Pop is livelier than soft rock, but not nearly as edgy as Rock. It's somewhere in between, it's modern, it's engaging and it definitely says "I'm here, I'm now, I'm ready."

Businesses that cater to young consumers may consider Pop, because it says:

Up-to-the-minute	Universal
Youthful	Earnest
Romantic	Modern
Fresh	Hip

Kinds of Businesses That Choose Pop Music

- Home furnishings and appliances
- Plastic and LASIK surgery
- Tourism
- Real estate
- Art galleries
- Restaurants
- Supermarkets

CHAPTER 33: R&B

Aretha Franklin, James Brown, Stevie Wonder, Kool & The Gang, Commodores, Tower of Power, TLC, Parliament. The music is contagious, the feeling is in the moment and the mood is upbeat.

Consider an R&B bed for businesses that want a youthful image that's:

Funky	Sexy
Outrageous	Partylike
Enthusiastic	Exuberant
Expressive	Passionate

Kinds of Businesses That Choose R&B Music

- Auto Dealers
- Window Coverings
- Restaurants
- Novelty shops
- Adult Entertainment
- TV/Electronics Stores
- Self-storage
- Casino
- Car Washes

CHAPTER 34: ROCK

Rolling Stones, Bruce Springsteen, Heart, Pat Benatar, Tom Petty, Pearl Jam, Alanis Morissette. When it's Rock, it's got hard edges. It's gritty, energetic and it's in your face. This is not the music for wallflowers. Rock is definitely *not* for businesses that want to keep a low profile.

On the other hand, Rock is a great music choice for businesses with a somewhat traditional "masculine" image or just businesses that want to convey an image that's:

Aggressive	Fierce
Proud	Confident
Bold	A cut above
Self-assured	Edgy

Kinds of Businesses That Choose Rock Music

- Trucks, convertibles, SUV Dealerships
- Convenience marts
- Bars and Clubs
- Auto detail and custom shops
- Audio and video equipment stores
- Sport and recreation venues
- Motorsports
- Universities

CHAPTER 35: SOFT ROCK

Billy Joel, Jewel, Norah Jones, Anita Baker, Phil Collins are the kinds of singers and composers who characterize the incredibly broad category of music known as "soft rock."

Also known as "Adult Contemporary," this style gets a workout in the world of jingles, because it's completely risk-free. Very few people actively dislike soft rock. That's not something that could be said of some of the other styles. Soft Rock tends to evoke feminine traits and is good for businesses that are:

Nurturing	Warm
Romantic	Trustworthy
Heartfelt	Genuine
Dependable	Compassionate

Kinds of Businesses That Choose Soft Rock Music

- Nursing and care facilities
- Hospitals, doctors, dentists and healthcare professionals
- Beauty salons
- Real Estate agents
- Financial institutions
- Nice restaurants
- Nonprofit and community organizations
- Jewelry stores

CHAPTER 36: ALL THE RIGHT WORDS

Lyrics and Wordplay

When a writer goes to work on fashioning your jingle, it may seem that he or she is just placing together words that sound good. Truth is, there's a lot of formal structure behind the way words go together to create a memorable jingle.

It's not necessarily important that you understand all of the technical aspects of how language works in lyrics, but if you're curious, read on.

You'll appreciate the songwriter's craft far more when you see the number of tools they have at their disposal and the ways they employ them as they put together a song that's customized just for you.

Rhyme

Rhyme is, of course, the first thing we think of when we think of lyrics and memorable music. Although there are many forms of rhyme, when most folks hear the word in the everyday world, they think of what professor types call "full end rhyme." That's a situation in which two words sound exactly alike, except for their first letter or sound.

- Race – Pace
- Bike – Like
- Sweets – Treats

If possible, rhyming lyrics with your company, business or brand name is the strongest way to use wordplay in lyrics.

Puns

Puns are a sort of wordplay. A pun relies on a word having more than one meaning, and the pun can therefore be read or understood in more than one way. Here are some great examples from ad campaigns through the years.

- **Moss Security®:** Alarmed? You should be.

- **Wyborowa® Vodka:** Enjoyed for centuries straight.

- **Pioneer®:** Everything you hear is true.

- **Range Rover®:** It's how the smooth take the rough.

- **Weight Watchers® Frozen Meals**: Taste. Not waist.

- **Barbados:** Barbados. Goodness. Gracious.

- **British Steel®:** British Steel: British mettle.

- **First National Bank of Chicago**: First relationships last.

- **Kodak® Gold:** Is your film as good as Gold?

- **Ritz® Crackers:** Nothing fitz like a Ritz.

- **John Deere® Tractors:** Nothing runs like a Deere.

- **Mumm's® Champagne:** One word captures the moment. Mumm's the word.

- **Money Magazine®:** Reap the rewards of Money.

- **Absolut® Vodka**: Absolut magic.

- **Citibank®:** Because the Citi never sleeps.

- **IBM®:** I think, therefore IBM.

- **Cutty Sark® Whisky:** Live a Cutty above.

- **Campari®:** You'll find there is no Camparison.

Alliteration

Alliteration is repeating the same first letter or sound in a series of words...like *Sold in Sixty Seconds*.

- Back to basics

- Balance the books

- Boom or bust

- Feast or Famine

- Monday morning

- Pay the price

- Two to tango
- Crispity crunchity
- Brilliant branding
- Brains and brawn

Assonance

Assonance is rather like alliteration. In assonance, two or more words repeat a sound, but in this case, it's a vowel sound (a, e, i, o or u) rather than a consonant sounds. Unlike a full rhyme, the last letters or final sound of each word is not the same.

Here are some examples of assonance.

- Boat load
- Sweeps week
- Deep green sea
- Bright smile
- Great lake
- Farther, harder

Catchphrases

Catchphrases are familiar phrases (usually from television, movies or radio) that make their way into common use. Their life span is generally short; you don't hear all that many people asking "Where's the Beef?" anymore, but millions did in the 1980s. Catchphrases tend to be well known across the board, and even if you and your friends aren't using them, chances are, your kids (or nieces and nephews) are.

If a catchphrase can be worked neatly into the lyrics of your jingle, it can form a fun, lighthearted backbone for your campaign.

Most popular catchphrases nowadays are originally spoken in a movie or a television show. Used correctly, they boost a jingle's memory factor because they're already well known. They needn't be used verbatim; in fact, a catchphrase can be more effective if it's adapted slightly by the business that's advertising.

Some popular catchphrases from the past:

- As if
- I hate it when that happens
- Make my day
- No way!
- You go, girl!
- Do bears bear? Do bees be?
- Yadda yadda yadda
- Come up and see me sometime
- D'oh!
- Good Grief
- Hasta La Vista, Baby
- I'll be back
- He! Could! Go! All! The! Way!
- Sweet!
- Eexxxxcellent!
- Make it so
- Not that there's anything wrong with that…
- Play it again, Sam
- You will be assimilated
- Resistance is futile
- Show me the money
- Up, up and away
- You look marvelous
- Bada Boom, Bada Bing!

The benefit of using a catchphrase as the basis or a part of your jingle is that you don't have to teach listeners something completely new. Instead, you're counting on their familiarity with the phrase to help get your message into their minds just a little faster; you're using something they've already heard in a different context.

But that familiarity can also be a double-edged sword. Catchphrases have real drawbacks to consider. First, if a catchphrase is too closely tied to a negatively perceived character or situation, it's likely to bring to mind a set of associations that wouldn't benefit your business. You wouldn't want to borrow "To the moon!" because of its association with Ralph Kramden in moments of pique (for obvious reasons). Likewise, although Bart Simpson's "eat my shorts" enjoyed wide popularity, it's hard to imagine an appropriate context for using it in a jingle.

☑ A Checklist: Do Any of These Words Sound Like Your Business?

bang	grrrr	skim
bong	gurgle	slap
babble	hack	slop
boing	ha-ha	slurp
bonk	he-ha	snap
boom	hiccup	sniffle
bop	hiss	splash
bump	honk	plunk
burp	humph	plink
buzz	hush	splat
brrrrr	jingle	sputter
chatter	meow	squeak
clack	moan	squish
clank	moo	tear
clap	mumble	tick-tock
clatter	murmur	thud
click	neigh	thump
cluck	oink	thunder
clip-clop	ooze	thunk jingle
crack	phew	tinkle
crash	ping	trickle
creak	plop	twinkle
coo	pop	ugh
crunch	pow	vroom
cuckoo	psst	wheeze
ding	quack	whirl
ding-dong	rattle	woof
drip	ribbit	whoop
eek	rip	yank
explode	rumble	yahoo
fizz	screech	wow
giggle	shhh	zap
goo goo gaa gaa	shimmy	zip
groan	sizzle	

Onomatopoeia

"Onomatopoeia" (pronounced *AH-no-MAH-toe-PEE-ah)* is a fifty-cent way of saying "a word or words that sound like what they're describing" While it's not always appropriate or necessary to include onomatopoeia in a jingle, where it can be used, it can be used to good effect.

Here are some great examples of Onomatopoeia. If any of them might help to drive home part of the message you want to convey about your business, you and your jingle composer should definitely work to incorporate them into your final jingle.

Rice Krispies®

It's fun to put
Snap!
Crackle!
Pop!
Into your morning

Alka Seltzer®

Plop, Plop
Fizz
Fizz
Oh what a relief it is

Slinky®

What walks down stairs
Alone or in pairs
And makes a slinkety sound?
A spring! A spring!
A marvelous thing
Everyone knows
It's Slinky!

CHAPTER 37: POSITIONING STATEMENTS AND SLOGANS

A Positioning Statement, also known as a slogan, should communicate the benefit or difference that separates your specific business, product or service from your competition. A slogan is literally meant to rally the troops.

Incidentally, the word "slogan" itself comes to the English language by way of the Irish *slogorne,* which meant "battle cry", from the Gaelic *sluagh ghairm,* meaning "army cry" or "cry to the multitude." Bet you didn't know that before, did you? Now, if only we could set it to music in this book, you'd always remember it.

The Positioning Statement is the rudder of your advertising and marketing, setting direction for your outreach efforts and keeping you on course.

An effective Positioning Statement:

- Is quickly understood, whether "seen" or "heard"
- Provides a consistent theme that ties all of your advertising together
- Builds consumer memory through repetition

In the world of local advertising, *recall* of your product or service at the time of a buying decision is the key. If your business, product or service is not the first or second one that comes into the consumer's mind at the time of a buying decision, the chances are great that you *won't* be the selected supplier.

Never Infringe A Known Registered Mark

Most Positioning Statements are born from commonly used phrases or words, and so we often see similar slogans (or slogan elements) used by more that one advertiser. Even in the national arena, both Coke and Wal-Mart® (use or have used) the Positioning Statement, "Always." In the case of these two huge corporations, both can use the same line because they are not in competing fields and there is little potential for the consumer to be "confused" by their use of similar slogans.

There are many occasions, however, especially with national products, when a Positioning Line has been "Registered" either as a service mark or trademark. In these instances, normal procedure is to put the public on notice with a ™, an ® or an "SM."

If a positioning line is already being used in your competitive space (the auto industry or restaurant business or toy retailing, etc.), you should strive to be sure your own slogan is completely different.

NEVER use a line that you know is some other party's intellectual property. The law protects those who have been granted "ownership" of a line. (On the other hand, it is very difficult to be granted registration for common words or phrases. Many times the only way a registration is granted is when the words are accompanied and combined with a unique graphic logo.)

A Slogan is Not Forever

In advertising, it is usually best to stay the course. You want customers to remember you for a long time, and you don't want to confuse them with ever-changing messages or positions.

That said, positioning statements CAN and DO change. Over the course of years, McDonald's has used a variety of slogans. "You deserve a break today"; "Two all beef patties, special sauce, lettuce, cheese, pickles, onions on a sesame seed bun"; "We love to see you smile"; and "I'm lovin' it" are just some of their slogans. They have the advertising budget to create and maintain evolving product awareness … and they apparently have had the need.

For local advertisers without McDonald's budget, however, we always advise that you should only change for a sound reason.

- Is there a new development in your business, product or service?

- Is the new thing what you want the consumer to concentrate on and remember about you?

- Is the new thing the thing that really and truly sets you apart from the competition?

If any of those things are true, then it might be time to create a new line that reflects the change.

CHAPTER 38: GETTING TO KNOW YOUR JINGLE

Congratulations: You've done it.

You've chosen to create a jingle that's going to do for your business what no amount of nonmusical advertising could ever do—get you into your potential customer's brain and keep you there.

When you work with a jingle production company, you should expect to receive a final CD that you can give to any local broadcast station for use in the ads you'll run for the next few years. On this CD, there will be several versions of your jingle.

The :60 Cut

Also known as a "Fullest Sing," the :60 (or sixty second) cut is an entire song, all by itself. In some :60s, there's no room for extra words or voiceovers, because the entire minute is full of lyrics. In others, the first :30 are entirely sung, leaving the final half-minute open for voiceover. This cut is not used often, but when it is, it can be a powerful tool. (We know of at least one :60 Fullest Sing jingle that had people calling in, requesting to hear the song.)

One great use of the :60 is to introduce your target market to your new jingle. If you play the :60 for a month or two by itself, they'll learn the whole song—and then when you scale back on the lyrics and run a :30, a donut or a sing-in, they'll mentally fill in the rest of the words themselves. You've just made your audience do some of the work for you!

The :30 Cut

Now that you know a :60 is a full minute long, you can probably guess what a :30 cut is. It's a half-minute and it's all lyrics. The :30 is a natural reinforcer once people know your :60 spot. Some businesses choose to begin by playing the :30 and never actually run the :60—this approach works too, so long as your lyrics have been tightly and carefully written and you can tell buyers all about your benefits in :30.

The Sing-In, Donut and Sing-Out

The sing-in is a cut of your jingle that begins with ten to fifteen seconds of lyrics—probably your business name and slogan—and then leaves a "blank" music bed for either live or locally recorded voiceovers promoting short-term specials or other information that changes often. You should expect to receive both :30 and :60 versions of a sing-in.

A sing-out, not surprisingly, is the opposite of a sing-in. Also called "instrumental-to-tag," it begins with lyric-less music and concludes with your name and slogan being sung. The instrumental-to-tag works best when folks already know your unique jingle; you don't have to use up precious airtime seconds to *tell* them who's advertising, because the music tells them that. Budweiser and United Airlines both use music alone to indicate an ad is theirs; the opening fanfare for Bud and Gershwin's "Rhapsody in Blue" have been used for so many years by these two national giants, they can use all of their airtime to deliver a targeted message without ever saying their name.

Finally, the donut is just what it sounds like—a :30 or :60 spot with a sing-in and sing-out, with the blank spot for voiceover smack dab in the middle. Again, it's most useful when you're running a promotion or offering specific information like special pricing for a limited time.

The Holiday, Theme or Promotional Sing

Your jingle producer can also produce variations on your jingle once you've settled on the basic melody and lyrics. Adding sleigh bells, chimes and other holiday instruments can spice up your ads during the critical winter shopping season. During Fourth of July promotions, many other styles of music can be recorded in a patriotic Anthem style, even including fireworks. A good producer can always make your "old" jingle sound fresh and new, adding great equity to your audio image and brand.

CHAPTER 39: USING YOUR JINGLE

So you've got a jingle. Now what?

Use it. Use it everywhere you possibly can. It's not just for radio anymore!

- **Local Cable advertising** is often quite affordable, and coupling your new, powerful audio image with great photography or video can really round out a picture for your potential buyers. You can use the Sing-in, the Donut, even the :60 and :30 full sing cuts effectively in cable advertising.

- **Do you have a Web Site?** Then give users the opportunity to hear your jingle when they visit your page—but be warned! Not everybody is going to love it quite as much as you, especially if the boss is wandering nearby, so you should give your users an immediate and obvious way to mute the sound on your page. You want customers to like you, not to feel like you're waiting to take them hostage. So give them the choice to listen—or not.

- **Music On Hold.** Your phone service may be able to turn your jingle into the background sound people hear when they're on hold for those few, scant seconds. It's better than dead air and usually a lot better than the insipid instrumental music we've grown to know and tolerate in, oh, say, elevators!

- **Overhead music systems.** The right kind of business can intersperse their own jingle into a mix of music coming from a CD player or other music source that plays in the retail space. But resist the temptation to overdo it: Once an hour is enough.

CHAPTER 40: JINGLE DO'S AND DON'TS

Do

- **Be inclusive.** Have everybody who'll be involved in the process available and present on every phone call to your jingle producer. Nothing is worse than picking something you like and developing lyrics and getting excited about it, then asking Mom what she thinks and suddenly hearing "I don't like it." If you want Mom's opinion to count, involve her at the outset.

- **Be open-minded** about various styles of music going in. You might not begin the process thinking that you'll settle on Blues, but it's possible that would be the perfect sound for your business.

- **Keep the team small.** Once you have more than about four people involved in a decision, reaching consensus becomes much more difficult. Narrow down the people you want to be involved to as few as possible—the ones who really matter and whom you really trust.

- **Know the roles** of the Advertising Agency, the Production Company and you as a business owner. Ultimately, both the agency and the production company are there to advise you and help you to realize *your* vision for your company—not to talk you into something you don't like or to tell you who you are.

- **Speak your mind early and often.** Any good jingle producer would rather have your candid opinion early in the process—it helps us to do better work for you.

- **Be prepared to have customers sing to you.** It happens a lot when a great new jingle gets rolled out.

- **Use your jingle** every way you can.

- **Have fun!**

Don't

- **Don't bring in new people midstream.** Once you've committed to a decision making team, stick with that team and make sure everybody is present during every consultation and call. Everybody wants their own opinion to be heard, and if somebody comes into the middle of the process, it's almost inevitable that they'll slow things down.

- **Don't tell the agency to handle it** unless you really want them to handle it. We've found that most of our clients through the years have ended up far happier if they participated in the jingle creation process—even the ones who initially said, "You take care of it" to their ad agency. The truth is, we all care about our image!

- **Don't worry about the technical things.** You know your business inside and out, and agencies and jingle producers know how to get that information out of you. You don't even have to worry about things like musical styles or lyrics—unless you really want to know the nitty-gritty details. Your jingle producer should always be willing to educate you if you want to understand the mechanics, but the best part for many business owners is that they don't need to spend time fretting about the technicalities of music production.

Chapter 41: More Homework

Worksheet 1: Honing in on Your Positioning Statement

By now you understand that for a Positioning Statement to be truly effective, the statement must be crafted to accomplish specific objectives.

Here is a worksheet that helps you to gather a lot of information that will be helpful as you work with your production company to produce the jingle that is uniquely you.

1. If you have a Mission Statement, write it below.

_____

_____

_____

_____

_____

2. Do you currently have or have you in the past used a "slogan" or "positioning statement? Look on your business cards, invoices, past radio commercials, your trucks etc. Look everywhere.

_____ *No. I don't have one and never had one.*

_____ *Yes. I used one in the past, but I have not used it recently.*

What was the line and when was it last used?

_____

_____

_____

_____

_____

_____ *Yes. I have one that I currently use.*

What is the line and how long have you been using it?

_____

_____

_____

_____

_____

3. If you answered "yes" to the above, what has changed in your business that either made you stop using your line or made you consider changing the line?

_____

_____

_____

_____

_____

4.When you first went into business, did you believe that you would "fill a void in your marketplace?"

_____ *No. I just like the field and wanted to be an additional alternative.*

_____*Yes. There was a definite need for my product, business or service.*

5. If you answered "No" to the above, then why do you believe that your business, product or service is the "best choice" that a consumer can make?

_____

_____

_____

_____

_____

6. If you answered "Yes" to Question 4, explain what is unique about your business, product or service that fills the need in the marketplace.

_____

_____

_____

_____

_____

7. What four words would best describe your company?

_____

_____

_____

_____

8. List the competitors in your marketplace and, if your competition uses a Positioning Line or slogan, please supply it.

_____

_____

_____

_____

_____

_____

_____

_____

9. Have fun with the following ... but *be truthful*. (Circle ONE on each line.)

Would _YOU_ describe your business as…

Filet Mignon	*Chicken*	*Spare Ribs*
Buick®	*Ferrari*®	*Jeep*® *4x4*
Aspen	*New Orleans*	*New York*
Frank Sinatra	*Aretha Franklin*	*Garth Brooks*
Red	*Yellow*	*Blue*
Collie	*Bulldog*	*Poodle*
Dog	*Cat*	*Show Horse*
Blonde	*Brunette*	*Redhead*

10. Would _your customer_ describe your product as:

Filet Mignon	*Chicken*	*Spare Ribs*
Buick	*Ferrari*	*Jeep 4x4*
Aspen	*New Orleans*	*New York*
Frank Sinatra	*Aretha Franklin*	*Garth Brooks*
Red	*Yellow*	*Blue*
Collie	*Bulldog*	*Poodle*
Dog	*Cat*	*Show Horse*
Blonde	*Brunette*	*Redhead*

11. If you could pick any celebrity spokesperson for your company, who would it be?

_____

12. If you could change one thing about your business, product or service, what would that one thing be?

_____
_____
_____
_____

Give this worksheet to your jingle producer and you'll be ready to roll.

CHAPTER 42: FIRST, A PLAN

Developing a plan to win more customers takes time, effort and a dedication that most new entrepreneurs or busy established businesses think they don't have.

But without a map to guide you to your ultimate destination, treacherous roadblocks and time-consuming detours can keep you from reaching your goals.

Try not to look at planning as a formality or obligation, but as something that can solve tangible problems like improving cash flow, generating new business, overcoming ill will and meeting customer deadlines. Planning is a way to solve problems before they arise. Don't leave your life or the success of your business to chance.

Planning doesn't stop once you open your business, close the deal or win the account. It's a constant process that demands concentration and hard work, but the payoff is worth it.

By applying the planning techniques that sophisticated public relations and marketing professionals use to position companies, promote causes or sell products, you can improve your business, advance your career and improve every other facet of your life.

Let's work at developing a rudimentary marketing plan. Marketing plays a vital role in successful business ventures, yet its systematic implementation is often overlooked by many small businesses.

Sure, every business owner has his repertoire of marketing gimmicks, but we've noticed over the years that the majority of small businesses operate without formal business plans, let alone a marketing strategy.

If you're one whose total marketing efforts include an ad in the yellow pages, some outdoor signage and an occasional flyer, this short marketing course is for you.

The Basics

Too many business owners concentrate on the tactical plan—jingles, radio ads, television ads, newspaper ads, billboards, newsletters, press kits, trade shows, banners, 800-numbers, display advertisements, logos and giveaways—before the strategic plan.

Those promotional, publicity and advertising tactics—and there are thousands to choose from—should be contained within a well-orchestrated marketing plan.

A marketing plan is a strategy best contained in a formal document, not on a cocktail napkin or recalled from memory. Approach this checklist as though you were compiling a simple report.

Each subsection requires an appropriate entry. You—the business owner—should write a few paragraphs for each topic. When finished, you'll have a basic marketing plan.

- The **executive summary** consists of a one-page top-level summary of the entire plan. It's placed at the front of the document, but it's the last thing you'll write. Its purpose is to convey the gist of the plan to stakeholders, investors and anyone else who needs to know the facts in a hurry.

- The **scope of the plan** is a paragraph that outlines the product or service being marketed, for whom the plan is being prepared, the time period the plan covers and the geographic area where the implementation occurs.

- The **firm profile** introduces the company and includes: a brief overview of the service; a brief overview of the personnel involved; a past history of the company; its present performance; and financial information if appropriate.

- The **service profile** provides information regarding the specific items you intend to market. By addressing the following categories, a profile emerges.
  - The **Positioning Statement** is the niche the product or service is intended to occupy.
  - The **Description** is your product or service described in detail.
  - **Pricing** covers the methods you use to determine how much you charge for goods or services.
  - **Market maturity** addresses whether this is a new service or product, an old one, and where it is in the cycle from introduction to retirement.

- **New market potential** is a rough approximation of the potential size of the local market for your products and services.
- **Delivery of service** describes how you actually do what you do—you explain the mechanisms of doing or selling.

- **Packaging** includes overall presentation of the product or service and its delivery.

- **Image** is the impression customers receive from employees, furnishings, stationary, etc. Image will be a top consideration when you create a jingle, so you should work through the worksheets at the end of the book to help you narrow this down as thoroughly as you can.

- It's important to identify the **target audience** or the customers you intend to reach. Provide specific information about the people your company considers its clients.

- It's also important to identify **user trends** or those changes in the market that can create opportunities for your company.

- A **brief summary** of past revenue performance should be given. Why do you think you were successful in the past? Look at issues related to growth, which include: seasonal sales performance, cyclical or repeating patterns and an evaluation of what has been done by others trying to market this type of product or service.

- The **type of competition** you face in the marketplace should be addressed. Insight here will help you understand why certain competitors have done so well (or so poorly) and why, and how your competition can create opportunities for you.

- An assumption of the **uncontrollable elements in the marketing environment** or what we call marketing considerations, should be offered. These assumptions include, for example, anticipation of radical changes in the social, political or economic environment. Hopefully, you'll be able to identify realistic challenges that you can expect to face in the marketplace.

- What are your **objectives?** What do you intend to accomplish in the next six months? One year? Five years? Elaborate on your marketing objectives and attempt to assign some kind of figure to market share, growth and market penetration.

- Next, the **tools, training and support** needed to accomplish the sales objectives—or what's called your lead conversion strategy—needs to be addressed.

- Last, you'll need to establish some type of budget to execute your marketing plan.

If you manage to write two or three paragraphs for each of the topics, you'll end up with at least a 10-page marketing plan. From there, you can refine your objectives. More important though, you've taken a big step forward because you've written your strategy down on paper.

As baseball great Yogi Berra once said, "If you don't know where you are going, you might not get there." But you're ahead of the game, because this marketing plan is your blueprint to success.

ABOUT THE AUTHORS

Ann McWilliams and David Mayo are two of the creative minds that make up Tuesday Productions, a southern California company that specializes in recording, producing, and licensing professional music and jingles for local and national broadcast advertisers.

They've helped more than 10,000 local, regional, and national advertisers set their message to music. Why? Because the ultimate aim of advertising is to be remembered, and music makes memories.

Tuesday has worked with thousands of local business owners to find just the right sound and lyrics. The result: Jingles that people just can't get out of their heads.

www.ingramcontent.com/pod-product-compliance
Lightning Source LLC
Chambersburg PA
CBHW022104170526
45157CB00004B/1484

* 9 7 8 1 4 2 0 8 5 2 6 1 5 *